The Grateful Hearts Givings Garden

The Grateful Hearts Givings Garden

Designing a Garden That Serves You for a Lifetime

By Joann Comer-Conwell

Copyright © 2026 JoAnn Comer-Conwell &

Grateful Hearts Givings NJ Nonprofit

All rights reserved.
No part of this book may be reproduced, stored in a retrieval system, or transmitted in any form or by any means—electronic, mechanical, photocopying, recording, or otherwise—without prior written permission of the author, except for brief quotations in reviews.

This book is sold subject to the condition that it shall not, by way of trade or otherwise, be lent, resold, hired out, or otherwise circulated without the publisher's prior consent in any form of binding or cover other than that in which it is published.

The information contained in this book is for educational purposes only. The author is not a medical professional, agricultural extension agent, or legal advisor. Readers are encouraged to use their own judgment and consult appropriate professionals when necessary. The author assumes no responsibility for errors, omissions, or outcomes resulting from the use of this information.

Scripture quotations are taken from the Holy Bible.
All scripture references are used for inspirational and educational purposes.

ISBN: 979-8-9993039-3-6
Printed in the United States of America

Dedication & Acknowledgments

Above all, I give thanks to God, whose design for provision was never meant to be complicated, fear-driven, or detached from relationship. This work exists because of His faithfulness, and it is offered with a grateful heart.

Most especially, this book is dedicated to my husband, Mike. He is the strength God gave me to do this work. Without his support, encouragement, and willingness to stand beside me through every garden, every season, and every challenge, not a single garden would have been built. His steadiness, protection, and love made this work possible, and I am deeply grateful for him.

This book is dedicated to every person who has ever looked at their plate and wondered where their food truly came from—and then felt called to do something about it. It is also dedicated to those who grow quietly, give generously, and work faithfully, often without recognition, including the helpers who lend their hands and the landowners who extend trust.

This work is carried out through Grateful Hearts Givings NJ Nonprofit, whose mission is rooted in feeding people with dignity, integrity, and compassion. Every garden, every lesson, and every harvest described in these pages reflects the purpose of this nonprofit—to grow food, build community, and serve others with grateful hearts.

I acknowledge the wisdom passed down through generations of gardeners who understood that food is not just nourishment for the body, but a responsibility of the heart.

Introduction

Gardening is often presented as something you must keep up with.
Keep planting. Keep lifting. Keep producing. Keep going.

But over time, I began to notice something different. The gardens that lasted were not the ones built with urgency or ambition. They were the ones designed with foresight. They belonged to people who planned not just for growth, but for change—change in health, time, energy, and circumstances.

This book exists because gardening should not require constant strength to be sustainable. A garden that demands more than it gives will eventually be abandoned, no matter how beautiful it once was.

This book explains how to design a giving garden that continues to function as physical ability, available time, and support systems change. It focuses on accessible garden systems, self-watering container design, and long-term food growing methods that support seniors, volunteers, and community food distribution without constant physical strain.

The Grateful Hearts Givings Garden introduces a different approach—one rooted in longevity rather than intensity. It is built on the idea that gardens should serve people across a lifetime, not just during peak seasons of ability.

While the phrase "garden like you're 80" introduced the method in the previous book, this volume clarifies what it always meant: not age, but foresight—designing in a way that honors every season of life.

Here, design choices are not made for appearance alone, but for accessibility, ease, and shared responsibility. Raised containers, self-watering systems, and thoughtful layouts are not shortcuts. They are expressions of wisdom.

This book is not about how much you can grow. It is about how long you can continue to grow without harm—to your body, your spirit, or your peace.

Welcome to
The Grateful Hearts Givings Garden

The Grateful Hearts Givings Garden

If you are holding this book, you are already someone who understands that gardening is more than growing plants. It is about care, patience, responsibility, and the quiet ways we tend both the land and one another.

The Grateful Hearts Givings Garden was written for those who want their gardens to remain a source of peace—not pressure—through every season of life. It is for those who have loved gardening deeply and want to keep loving it without exhaustion. It is also for those who are just beginning and want to build something that will last.

This book does not ask you to work harder.
It asks you to think more gently.

Here, gardening is approached as a relationship rather than a task. A relationship that changes over time, requires wisdom instead of force, and benefits from systems that support the gardener as much as the plants.

You will not find rules meant to impress or techniques designed to push your limits. What you will find are design principles rooted in lived experience—principles that make gardens easier to care for, safer to work in, and more open to sharing with others.

At the heart of this garden is the belief that sustainability includes people.

A garden that cannot be maintained without strain is not sustainable.

A garden that cannot be shared cannot truly serve.
And a garden that demands constant effort will eventually be abandoned.

The Grateful Hearts Givings Garden is about designing spaces that endure. Spaces that invite help. Spaces that forgive absence. Spaces that continue to give even when life becomes busy, bodies grow tired, or circumstances change.

As you move through these pages, take your time. Notice what resonates. Allow yourself to question long-held assumptions. And above all, give yourself permission to design a garden that serves you well—now and for years to come.

You are welcome here.

A Note from the Author

I didn't set out to create a system. I set out to keep gardening possible.

Over time, I noticed how often people—including myself—designed gardens that depended on strength, speed, and constant effort. And I watched how quietly those gardens became burdens when life shifted, health changed, or help was needed.

What changed everything for me was learning to design with foresight instead of urgency.

The ideas in this book were shaped through real gardens, real seasons, and real limitations. They were refined through caring for others, sharing food, and building systems that had to work even when I couldn't give them my full attention.

This book reflects what I have endured.

My hope is that what you find here helps you design a garden that remains kind—to your body, to your time, and to the people who may one day step in beside you.

Thank you for being here.

— JoAnn Comer-Conwell

How to Use This Book

This book is designed to be read slowly.

It is not a manual to complete or a system to master. Each chapter builds understanding through reflection, design awareness, and practical observation. You may read straight through or pause between chapters as needed.

Every chapter follows the same rhythm, allowing ideas to settle and connect naturally:

Opening Reflection introduces the design principle through lived experience.
The Hidden Problem names what quietly undermines sustainability.
The Design Shift reframes the way the garden is understood.
The Grateful Hearts Solution shows how thoughtful design restores balance.
Design Truth clarifies what lasts beyond technique.
Practical Pause invites honest observation without pressure.
Bringing It Together integrates the idea into the larger purpose of the garden.

You do not need to apply everything at once. This book is meant to inform decisions over time, allowing your garden to evolve as your life does.

A Note on Pace

You may feel tempted to skip ahead to the practical sections. That's natural. But the foundation matters here. This book is not about adding tasks—it is about removing strain. The early chapters shape the way you think before they ask you to build or change anything.

Move slowly. Revisit sections. Let ideas settle before acting on them.

Understanding the Chapter Structure

Every chapter in this book follows the same rhythm. This repetition is intentional. Familiar structure allows your mind to rest so your attention can deepen.

Each chapter includes:

- The Opening
- The Grateful Hearts Givings Principle
- What You Need to Know
- The Hard Truth
- How This Looks in Real Life
- Scripture in Practice
- Garden Wisdom
- Bringing It Together
- Pause & Reflect

You do not need to complete every section in one sitting. Some readers pause at the Hard Truth. Others linger in Garden Wisdom. There is no correct order beyond attentiveness.

Using This Book in Real Time

You can read this book alongside your garden—or long before you ever plant anything.

If you are currently gardening, use the Pause & Reflect sections to evaluate what is working and what feels heavy.
If you are planning a garden, let the early chapters guide your design decisions before you commit to materials or layouts.
If you are no longer able to garden as you once did, this book will help you reimagine what is still possible.

A Gentle Reminder

This book is not a test of productivity or commitment.

A garden that serves you well is one that allows for rest, interruption, and shared responsibility. If at any point the process begins to feel burdensome, step back. Reread. Reflect. Adjust.

That, too, is good stewardship.

Chapter One

Gardening Is Not About Age

Gardening is often described as something people grow out of—as if time itself makes soil heavier, beds lower, and harvests harder to reach. When gardens become difficult to maintain, age is usually blamed first.

But age is not what ends most gardens.

Long before birthdays matter, gardens begin to fail because they were designed around strength instead of sustainability. They were built for the season of enthusiasm, not the seasons that follow. They assumed constant energy, perfect health, and uninterrupted time.

Age does not cause gardens to become difficult. It simply reveals whether the design was thoughtful enough to last.

The Hidden Problem

The hidden problem is not growing older. It is designing gardens that require more effort every year just to remain functional. Lifting water. Bending low. Carrying heavy soil. Reaching awkwardly. These demands quietly accumulate until the joy that once fueled the work is replaced by strain.

When people hear the phrase *"garden like you're 80,"* it is easy to misunderstand what is being asked. Some hear limitation. Others hear exclusion. But the phrase was never meant to describe age. It was meant to expose a truth that applies to every gardener, at every stage of life.

The Design Shift

Gardening is not about preparing for old age.
It is about preparing for real life.

Bodies change. Schedules change. Seasons interrupt plans. Illness, caregiving, work, and weather all arrive without permission. A garden that only works when everything goes right is not resilient. It is fragile.

The design shift happens when we stop asking how much we can do and start asking what will continue to work when we cannot.

The Grateful Hearts Solution

The Grateful Hearts approach begins with a simple question: **Will this garden still serve me if my energy changes, my time becomes limited, or someone else needs to step in?**

If the answer is no, the issue is not commitment or discipline. The issue is design.

Gardens designed with foresight do not depend on constant effort. They rely on structure, placement, and systems that support consistency without exhaustion. Raised containers reduce strain. Self-watering systems remove daily urgency. Clear paths allow others to help without instruction.

These choices are not shortcuts.
They are expressions of wisdom.

Design Truth

A well-designed garden does not assume decline.
It simply refuses to depend on strength alone.

It honors the future gardener by making the work lighter before it becomes heavy.

Gardening has never been about age.
It has always been about whether the garden serves the gardener—or the gardener serves the garden.

Practical Pause

Before moving forward, pause and observe your own space.

Notice where effort feels unnecessary.
Notice what requires the most physical strain.
Notice what would be difficult for someone else to understand or maintain.

These observations are not criticisms.
They are information.

Bringing It Together

When design comes first, age becomes irrelevant. The garden adapts. It waits. It continues.

A garden that lasts is not built on endurance.
It is built on kindness extended into the future.

And that is where this garden begins.

Bringing It Together

Chapter Two

The Cost of Overbuilding

Most gardens are built with enthusiasm at full strength.

Big plans. Big beds. Big promises.

At the beginning, overbuilding looks like abundance. It feels productive, impressive, even faithful. But time has a way of revealing what enthusiasm hides. What once felt generous can quietly become heavy. What once felt manageable can begin to ask more than it gives.

Overbuilding rarely feels like a mistake in the moment it happens. It feels like hope.

The Hidden Problem

The hidden problem with overbuilding is not the work itself. It is the assumption behind it.

Overbuilt gardens assume that energy will remain constant, that time will always be available, that bodies will cooperate, and that life will not interrupt. They assume that the gardener will always be present in the same way, with the same strength and capacity.

But gardens do not exist in isolation. They exist inside real lives. Lives that change. Bodies that tire. Seasons that shorten. Responsibilities that shift.

When a garden is built larger than the margin of life allows, it begins to pull instead of serve.

The Design Shift

The design shift begins with a simple question:
What does this garden require from me to keep going?

Not at its best.
Not in peak season.
But on ordinary days, tired days, interrupted days.

Designing wisely means resisting the urge to grow everything at once. It means choosing restraint not as limitation, but as protection. A smaller, well-designed garden can outproduce a large one that cannot be sustained.

This shift moves the gardener from proving capability to preserving capacity.

The Grateful Hearts Solution

The Grateful Hearts approach does not eliminate abundance. It reframes it.

Instead of expanding outward, it strengthens inward. Modular systems contained growing spaces, and intentional limits allow the garden to remain faithful without becoming fragile.

Overbuilding is replaced with rightsizing. Growth becomes intentional rather than impulsive. Each element is chosen because it earns its place through service, not ambition.

The garden becomes something that fits into life, not something life must bend around.

Design Truth

A garden that is too large to tend consistently will eventually be too large to love.

Overbuilding often leads to guilt rather than joy. Missed harvests, neglected beds, and constant catching up erode peace. The cost is not just physical effort. It is the quiet loss of confidence and delight.

Design truth reminds us that stewardship includes knowing when enough is enough.

Practical Pause

Consider the spaces you tend now.

Which areas feel light and satisfying?
Which ones feel heavy or urgent?
Which parts of your garden would continue with grace if you stepped back for a week?

This pause is not about judgment. It is about listening. Gardens speak clearly when we give them room to tell the truth.

Bringing It Together

Overbuilding is rarely about greed. It is about good intentions without design boundaries.

The Grateful Hearts Givings Garden teaches that longevity is not created by doing more, but by choosing wisely. A garden built within the limits of real life becomes a place of rest instead of pressure.

When a garden no longer demands constant proving, it becomes what it was always meant to be—a quiet partner, not a relentless task.

Chapter Three

Designing for the Season You're In

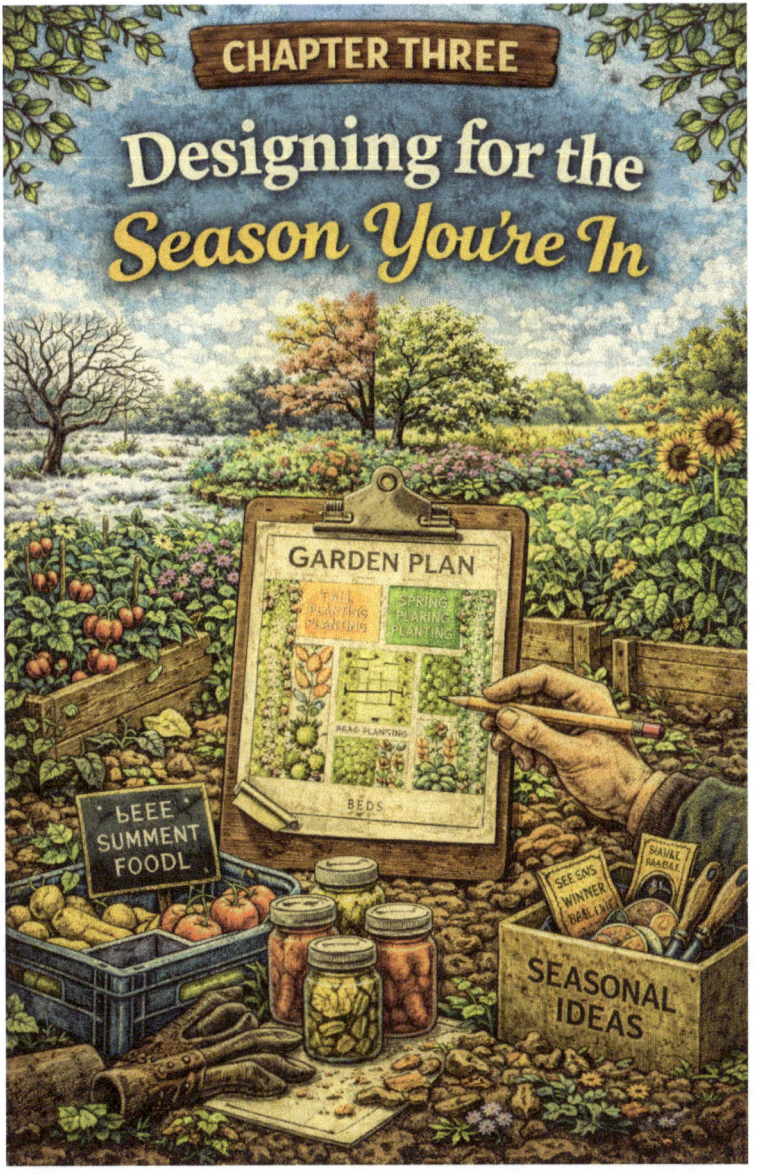

Every garden exists in a season, whether we acknowledge it or not.

Some seasons are full—long days, strong bodies, eager hands. Others are quieter, marked by limited time, reduced energy, or responsibilities that pull attention elsewhere. The mistake is not having seasons. The mistake is designing as though seasons never change.

Many gardens are built during seasons of optimism. Energy is high. Plans are ambitious. The future feels distant. But gardens do not stay frozen in the moment they are built. They move forward, just as people do.

A garden designed without regard for season will eventually demand a version of you that no longer exists.

The Hidden Problem

The hidden problem is not aging, illness, or busyness.
The problem is denial.

Gardeners are often taught to build for their best season—when they have the most strength, the most time, the most motivation. That approach quietly assumes that this season will last. When it doesn't, the garden becomes a reminder of what can no longer be maintained.

This is why so many gardens fail not in winter, but in life transitions. A job changes. A body changes. A family need arises. The garden remains fixed while the gardener moves on.

What was once a joy becomes pressure.

The Design Shift

The design shift happens when you stop asking, "What can I handle right now?"
and begin asking, "What will still work when this season changes?"

Designing for the season you're in does not mean limiting yourself. It means choosing flexibility over permanence. It means building systems that can scale up or down without collapsing.

Modular beds, manageable planting zones, simple watering systems, and realistic crop choices are not signs of low ambition. They are signs of wisdom. They allow the garden to adjust when life does.

A garden designed with season in mind does not punish the gardener for needing rest.

The Grateful Hearts Solution

The Grateful Hearts Givings Garden is designed to meet people where they are—and stay with them as they move forward. It does not assume endless capacity. It assumes change.

This approach allows a garden to function during busy seasons and quiet ones. It allows productivity without pressure. It allows help to enter naturally, because the design is understandable and accessible to others.

When a garden is designed for the current season, with room for future ones, it becomes steady instead of fragile.

Design Truth

Gardens fail when they are designed for a version of life that no longer exists.

A design that honors season does not resist change. It anticipates it. It leaves space. It reduces complexity. It chooses systems that forgive missed days and imperfect care.

This is not settling.
This is stewardship.

Practical Pause

Consider the season you are in right now—not the one you wish you were in, and not the one you were in before.

How much time do you realistically have?
How much energy do you want to give without strain?
What would happen if the season shifted suddenly?

Designing honestly today protects peace tomorrow.

Bringing It Together

A garden designed for the season you're in will still be standing when the season passes. It will not demand explanations. It will not shame you for stepping back.

Instead, it will wait—quietly, faithfully—ready to serve again when the next season arrives.

That is the kind of garden meant to last.

Chapter Four

Reach, Lift, Bend, Repeat

Most gardening fatigue does not come from one hard day.

It comes from repetition.
Reaching for the same low bed.
Lifting the same heavy container.
Bending again and again without support or relief.
These movements seem small in isolation, but gardens are built on repetition. What the body does once, it will be asked to do hundreds of times over a season. When a garden ignores that reality, strain becomes inevitable.

A garden should not wear down the person tending it.

The Hidden Problem

The hidden problem is not weakness.
It is cumulative demand.

Many gardens are designed as though the body resets each day. They assume yesterday's bending does not affect today's reach. They ignore how joints remember, how backs tighten, how balance changes over time.

The result is not sudden injury, but quiet exhaustion. Gardening becomes something that requires recovery instead of restoration.

When the body begins to resist the work, the garden is often blamed. In truth, the design is asking too much.

The Design Shift

The design shift begins when you observe movement instead of effort.

Where do you reach most often?
What do you lift repeatedly?
How many times do you bend in a single visit to the garden?

Designing for movement means reducing unnecessary repetition. It means placing frequently used plants within easy reach. It means choosing lighter containers, higher growing surfaces, and layouts that allow standing work instead of constant bending.

This shift does not remove work. It removes strain.

The Grateful Hearts Solution

The Grateful Hearts Givings Garden treats the body as a long-term partner, not a temporary tool.

Raised and modular systems reduce bending. Self-watering containers reduce lifting. Clear pathways reduce awkward reaches and unstable footing. Each choice quietly protects the body from doing more than it should.

This design allows gardening to remain a steady practice instead of a physical challenge to overcome.

When the body is respected, consistency becomes possible.

Design Truth

A garden that relies on repeated strain will eventually be avoided.

Designing for reach, lift, and bend is not about making gardening easy. It is about making it sustainable. It acknowledges that bodies change, even when passion does not.

Wise design preserves both.

Practical Pause

Stand where you usually garden and notice your movements.

What do you reach for most often?
What feels heavy by the end of the day?
What motion makes you hesitate before repeating it?

Those hesitations are signals. A garden that listens to them can be adjusted before harm is done.

Bringing It Together

A garden that reduces unnecessary strain becomes a place of return, not recovery.

When reaching is easy, lifting is manageable, and bending is minimized, the garden stays inviting. It remains a space where work feels purposeful instead of punishing.

That kind of design allows gardening to continue—not just for a season, but for years to come.

Chapter Five

Height Is Mercy

Height determines how a garden is experienced long before a single seed is planted.

It decides whether you lean in with ease or brace yourself before approaching. It determines whether your hands meet the soil naturally or after strain. Height quietly dictates whether gardening feels welcoming or demanding.

When height is ignored, the body pays the price. When height is chosen wisely, the garden becomes an act of mercy.

The Hidden Problem

The hidden problem is the assumption that lower is better.

Traditional garden advice often praises ground-level planting as natural or authentic. But authenticity loses its value when it requires constant bending, kneeling, or reaching beyond comfort. What begins as a design choice slowly becomes a barrier.

Over time, low beds ask the gardener to compensate—to kneel longer, bend deeper, or push through discomfort. Eventually, even brief garden visits feel like a physical negotiation.

The garden does not change. The body does.

The Design Shift

The design shift occurs when height is treated as a support, not an indulgence.

Raising growing surfaces brings the garden to the gardener instead of forcing the gardener to descend repeatedly. It allows hands to work at a natural level and eyes to observe without strain.

This shift is not about eliminating effort. It is about placing effort where it belongs—in tending plants, not managing pain.

The Grateful Hearts Solution

The Grateful Hearts Givings Garden embraces height as a form of care.

Raised containers, elevated beds, and modular systems allow gardeners to choose what works best for their bodies. Height becomes adjustable rather than fixed, intentional rather than assumed.

These choices protect energy. They preserve joints. They allow gardening to remain a source of nourishment instead of fatigue.

When height is merciful, the garden becomes accessible again.

Design Truth

What you raise today determines what you can tend tomorrow.

A garden designed at the right height does not demand resilience. It offers partnership. It allows work to continue even when flexibility decreases or balance changes.

Designing with mercy extends the life of both the garden and the gardener.

Practical Pause

Stand beside your current growing spaces and notice where your hands naturally fall.

Is the work happening above, below, or at that level?
Where does your body tense automatically?
What height feels neutral instead of effortful?

Those observations reveal where mercy is missing—and where it can be restored.

Bringing It Together

Height is not a convenience. It is a commitment to longevity.

When a garden meets the body where it is, gardening becomes sustainable rather than seasonal. It remains something you return to willingly, not something you recover from afterward.

A garden designed with mercy allows care to continue—quietly, steadily, and without harm.

Chapter Six

Water Is the Hidden Labor

Water is often treated as the simplest part of gardening.

Turn on the hose. Fill the can. Move on.

But water is not simple. It is repetitive, constant, and quietly demanding. It asks to be carried, lifted, poured, remembered, and returned to again and again. Long after planting is finished, water continues the work.

What looks effortless on the surface is often the most exhausting task underneath.

The Hidden Problem

The hidden problem is not watering plants. It is moving water.

Buckets strain wrists. Hoses pull shoulders. Trips back and forth add up long before anyone notices the toll. Over time, watering becomes the task most likely to be delayed, rushed, or avoided altogether.

When watering becomes labor-heavy, consistency suffers. And when consistency suffers, the garden follows.

This is how gardens fail quietly—not from neglect, but from fatigue.

The Design Shift

The design shift happens when water is treated as infrastructure instead of effort.

Rather than asking the gardener to deliver water repeatedly, the garden is designed to hold, distribute, and manage it. Systems replace strain. Placement replaces hauling.

Water becomes something the garden receives naturally, not something the gardener must wrestle into place.

The Grateful Hearts Solution

The Grateful Hearts Givings Garden removes water from the list of daily burdens.

Self-watering containers, reservoirs, and gravity-assisted systems allow plants to access moisture steadily without constant human intervention. The gardener's role shifts from carrier to caretaker.

This approach protects energy and preserves consistency. It allows the garden to remain healthy even on days when strength, time, or weather is limited.

Water becomes supportive rather than exhausting.

Design Truth

A garden that depends on constant lifting will eventually outpace its gardener.

When water is built into the design, the garden becomes resilient. It continues through heat, fatigue, and missed days without crisis.

Designing for water management is not about convenience. It is about endurance.

Practical Pause

Notice how water moves through your current garden.

Where is it stored?
How often is it carried?
Which motions repeat the most?

Pay attention to the task you delay most often. That is where the hidden labor lives.

Bringing It Together

When water no longer requires strength, the garden regains stability.

Designing water systems that work quietly in the background allows the gardener to remain present without being depleted. The garden becomes forgiving instead of demanding.

A garden that manages its own water is a garden that understands service—and gives it back in return.

Chapter Seven

The Myth of Low Maintenance

Low maintenance is one of the most promised and least delivered ideas in gardening.

It appears on labels, websites, and advice meant to reassure. It suggests ease, simplicity, and freedom from effort. But most gardeners discover quickly that "low maintenance" often means something else entirely.

It usually means maintenance deferred, not removed.

The Hidden Problem

The hidden problem is the belief that gardens can be built once and then ignored.

In reality, gardens are living systems. When maintenance is postponed rather than designed for, it does not disappear. It accumulates. What is avoided early becomes overwhelming later.

Low maintenance is often achieved by pushing responsibility onto the future gardener—who is assumed to be just as capable, available, and energetic as the present one.

That assumption rarely holds.

The Design Shift

The design shift occurs when maintenance is treated as a design responsibility rather than a personal failure.

Instead of asking how to eliminate care, the question becomes how to distribute it gently over time. Good design reduces urgency, simplifies tasks, and prevents buildup.

Maintenance becomes smaller, steadier, and less disruptive. The garden no longer demands bursts of effort to recover from neglect.

The Grateful Hearts Solution

The Grateful Hearts Givings Garden does not promise low maintenance. It promises manageable maintenance.

Self-watering systems reduce daily attention. Modular beds limit the spread of problems. Thoughtful plant choices prevent constant correction. Clear layouts allow issues to be seen early, before they require heavy intervention.

Maintenance becomes part of the rhythm rather than an interruption to it.

This approach protects both the garden and the gardener from burnout.

Design Truth

There is no such thing as a garden without maintenance.

There are only gardens where maintenance is anticipated and gardens where it is postponed. One supports continuity. The other creates crisis.

Design truth teaches that sustainability comes from honesty, not illusion.

Practical Pause

Think about the tasks you postpone most often.

What feels too big to start?
What seems to pile up quickly?
What maintenance do you dread instead of accept?

Those answers point directly to design choices that need adjustment.

Bringing It Together

A sustainable garden is not one that asks for nothing. It is one that asks reasonably.

When maintenance is built into the design, it becomes lighter, predictable, and less disruptive. The garden remains steady instead of swinging between neglect and overwork.

Letting go of the myth of low maintenance makes room for something better—a garden that can be cared for without strain, season after season.

Chapter Eight

Containers That Work With You

Containers are often treated as temporary solutions.

They are seen as substitutes for "real" gardens or compromises made when space is limited. But containers, when chosen and designed well, offer something traditional beds often cannot—flexibility.

A container does not insist on permanence. It can be moved, adjusted, replaced, or rested. It responds to change instead of resisting it.

That responsiveness is not a weakness. It is strength.

The Hidden Problem

The hidden problem is not using containers.
It is choosing containers that work against the gardener.

Heavy pots that cannot be lifted. Containers without reservoirs that dry out too quickly. Designs that require constant monitoring and correction. These choices turn flexibility into frustration.

When containers demand more attention than the gardener can give, they lose their purpose. What should simplify the garden instead multiplies effort.

The Design Shift

The design shift happens when containers are chosen for partnership rather than appearance.

A container that works with you supports consistency. It holds moisture, balances weight and fits naturally into the flow of your space. It allows plants to thrive without constant intervention.

This shift moves the gardener from reacting to needs toward trusting systems that quietly do their work.

Containers stop being something you manage and become something you rely on.

The Grateful Hearts Solution

The Grateful Hearts Givings Garden embraces containers as long-term tools, not short-term fixes.

Modular, self-watering containers allow gardeners to scale up or down without disruption. Milk-crate systems, lightweight materials, and contained soil volumes make care predictable and accessible.

These containers invite help rather than complicate it. Anyone can understand how they function. Anyone can step in and support the garden without fear of doing harm.

That simplicity is intentional.

Design Truth

Containers reveal design honesty.

When chosen well, they make gardening lighter. When chosen poorly, they expose strain quickly. A container that must be constantly adjusted is not serving its purpose.

Design truth reminds us that flexibility must be paired with stability. Containers should respond to life, not demand attention from it.

Practical Pause

Look closely at the containers you use now.

Which ones feel easy to care for?
Which ones dry out fastest or feel heaviest to manage?
Which containers could be moved, rested, or rearranged without stress?

Those answers show which containers are working with you—and which are not.

Bringing It Together

Containers that work with you allow the garden to remain adaptable.

They make room for changing seasons, changing spaces, and changing needs. They allow growth without overcommitment and care without exhaustion.

A garden built with supportive containers becomes resilient by design—ready to adjust, ready to serve, and ready to continue.

Chapter Nine

Soil Is a Long-Term Relationship

Soil is often treated as a starting point.

It is purchased, poured, planted into, and forgotten. Attention shifts to what grows above the surface while what supports it below is assumed to remain the same. But soil remembers every choice made about it. It responds to care, neglect, and time.

A garden's future is written in its soil long before the harvest is visible.

The Hidden Problem

The hidden problem is the belief that soil can be replaced instead of tended.

When soil is treated as disposable, effort increases. Nutrients are chased. Problems are corrected repeatedly rather than prevented. The gardener works harder while the soil grows weaker.

This cycle creates dependence on constant inputs and constant correction. What should stabilize the garden instead becomes another source of labor.

Soil exhaustion rarely announces itself. It shows up as struggle.

The Design Shift

The design shift occurs when soil is treated as a relationship rather than a resource.

Healthy soil is built, not purchased repeatedly. It is protected from compaction, erosion, and depletion. It is allowed to improve over time rather than reset each season.

Designing for soil longevity means choosing contained systems, consistent amendments, and gentle care. It means disturbing soil less and supporting it more.

When soil is trusted, the garden becomes steadier.

The Grateful Hearts Solution

The Grateful Hearts Givings Garden treats soil as something to be kept, not replaced.

Self-contained growing systems protect soil structure. Compost is added thoughtfully rather than reactively. Soil volume is respected, allowing roots to establish without stress.

This approach reduces intervention. It allows the soil to do its work quietly, season after season.

A garden built on cared-for soil asks less and gives more.

Design Truth

Plants depend on soil more than gardeners realize.

When soil is healthy, plants resist stress, recover faster, and require less correction. When soil is depleted, every problem becomes urgent.

Design truth reminds us that soil stewardship is long-term thinking made visible.

Practical Pause

Consider how you currently treat your soil.

Is it reused or replaced?
Is it protected or compacted?
Does it improve each season or start over?

These questions reveal whether the relationship is being nurtured or neglected.

Bringing It Together

Soil does not demand perfection. It responds to consistency.

When soil is cared for as a long-term partner, the garden gains stability. Growth becomes reliable instead of reactive. Effort becomes lighter because the foundation is strong.

A garden that honors its soil is a garden designed to last.

Chapter Ten

A Garden Others Can Help In

Many people say they want help in the garden.

But wanting help and being able to receive it are not the same thing. A garden can be generous in intention and still impossible for others to enter. Complexity, confusion, and unspoken rules quietly turn willing hands away.

A garden that cannot be shared cannot truly be helped.

The Hidden Problem

The hidden problem is not a lack of volunteers.
It is a lack of design clarity.

Gardens are often built around one person's habits, memory, and strength. Paths make sense only to the builder. Systems rely on knowledge that lives in one mind. When others step in, they hesitate—not because they don't care, but because they don't want to cause harm.

This turns help into risk. And when helping feels risky, people step back.

The Design Shift

The design shift begins when a garden is built to be understood, not explained.

Clear paths, visible systems, and simple layouts remove uncertainty. When someone can see where to step, where to water, and where to harvest without instruction, participation becomes natural.

Designing for help means letting go of control and choosing clarity instead.

The Grateful Hearts Solution

The Grateful Hearts Givings Garden is designed with shared hands in mind.

Modular beds define responsibility. Self-watering systems remove guesswork. Accessible heights and open pathways invite entry without fear. Nothing is hidden. Nothing is fragile.

This design allows help to arrive without supervision. It transforms goodwill into action.

A garden built for others becomes a place of cooperation rather than caution.

Design Truth

Help is invited by design, not by request.

When a garden depends on one person's presence, it remains vulnerable. When it is designed for shared care, it becomes resilient.

Design truth teaches that dignity includes allowing others to contribute without confusion or correction.

Practical Pause

Imagine someone stepping into your garden without you.

Would they know where to walk?
Would they understand what needs care?
Would they feel confident enough to help without asking?

If not, the design may be unintentionally keeping people out.

Bringing It Together

A garden others can help in becomes more than a growing space.

It becomes a place where responsibility is shared, where care is multiplied, and where no single person carries the full weight. When design removes barriers, help becomes a gift instead of a burden.

That is how gardens endure—not through independence, but through thoughtful invitation.

Chapter Eleven

Growing Enough Without Growing Too Much

Abundance is often measured by volume.

More beds. More plants. More harvest. More to manage.

In gardening, growth is usually celebrated without question. But abundance without boundaries quietly becomes excess. What begins as provision can slowly turn into pressure when the garden produces more than can be cared for, harvested, or shared with intention.

Enough is not the same as more.

The Hidden Problem

The hidden problem is the belief that generosity requires expansion.

Gardeners often grow beyond their capacity because they want to give, provide, or prepare. But when growth outpaces the ability to tend, harvest, and distribute, the garden begins to strain the very purpose it was meant to serve.

Food goes unharvested. Beds become overwhelming. Guilt replaces gratitude.

The problem is not generosity. It is scale without design.

The Design Shift

The design shift happens when abundance is redefined.

Instead of measuring success by quantity, the focus moves to consistency and use. A garden designed to grow enough does not chase maximum yield. It prioritizes what can be sustained, enjoyed, and shared without exhaustion.

This shift allows the garden to remain faithful to its purpose without demanding constant expansion.

The Grateful Hearts Solution

The Grateful Hearts Givings Garden grows with intention.

Planting choices are made based on realistic harvest capacity and actual need. Modular systems allow production to increase or decrease without disrupting the whole garden. Nothing is planted simply because space is available.

This approach protects both the harvest and the gardener. It allows abundance to remain a blessing instead of becoming a burden.

Design Truth

A garden that produces more than can be handled creates waste, not provision.

True abundance is measured by use, not volume. When growth is aligned with capacity, the garden remains joyful and purposeful.

Design truth reminds us that restraint is not scarcity. It is stewardship.

Practical Pause

Reflect on what you grow most.

What do you harvest fully and consistently?
What is often left behind or rushed?
What produces more than you can reasonably manage?

Those answers reveal where "too much" may be hiding behind good intentions.

Bringing It Together

Growing enough honors both the land and the gardener.

When a garden is designed to match real capacity, it becomes sustainable and generous at the same time. Nothing is wasted. Nothing is overwhelming. Care and harvest remain balanced.

A garden that grows enough—without growing too much—serves with clarity, peace, and purpose.

Find our Journal on Amazon

By Joann Comer-Conwell

Chapter Twelve

Paths, Access, and Permission

How a garden is entered often determines how it is used.

Paths signal where to walk, where to pause, and where care is welcome. When access is unclear or difficult, even well-intentioned people hesitate. They slow down, step back, or avoid entering altogether.

A garden that is hard to move through quietly teaches people to stay out.

The Hidden Problem

The hidden problem is not space.
It is unintentional exclusion.

Narrow walkways, uneven ground, hidden edges, and unclear boundaries turn simple movement into uncertainty. People worry about stepping on plants, damaging beds, or getting in the way. When access feels risky, help disappears.

Gardens often assume familiarity. Visitors do not have it.

The Design Shift

The design shift begins when movement is treated as part of the garden's purpose.

Clear paths invite confidence. Defined edges remove doubt. Accessible spacing allows people to enter without asking permission. Design communicates where help is welcome and where care belongs.

When access is intentional, participation becomes natural.

The Grateful Hearts Solution

The Grateful Hearts Givings Garden is designed to be entered.

Paths are wide enough to walk comfortably. Surfaces are stable and visible. Growing areas are clearly defined without being closed off. Nothing requires special knowledge to navigate.

This design gives quiet permission. It tells others, without words, that they are allowed to be here and to help.

Design Truth

Access is an invitation.

When people can move easily, they engage willingly. When they cannot, even the most generous intentions remain unused. A garden that welcomes movement welcomes care.

Design truth reminds us that dignity includes making room.

Practical Pause

Walk through your garden as if you were seeing it for the first time.

Where would you hesitate?
What feels unclear or tight?
Where would you worry about causing damage?

Those moments point directly to places where access can be improved.

Bringing It Together

Paths do more than connect spaces. They connect people to purpose.

When a garden is designed with access in mind, it becomes open, usable, and shared. Movement becomes easy. Help becomes possible. Care becomes communal.

A garden that grants permission through design becomes a place where people can enter, contribute, and belong.

Chapter Thirteen

When You Miss a Day, a Week, a Season

Every gardener misses time.

A day slips by. A week passes unexpectedly. Sometimes a whole season arrives and leaves without attention. Life does not ask permission before interrupting care.

What matters is not whether time is missed, but how the garden responds when it is.

The Hidden Problem

The hidden problem is the belief that a good garden requires constant presence.

Many gardens are designed to need daily attention. Water must be delivered. Weeds must be caught immediately. Harvest must happen at just the right moment. When the gardener steps away, even briefly, the system begins to unravel.

This creates pressure. Gardening becomes something that cannot be paused without consequence.

The Design Shift

The design shift happens when forgiveness is built into the garden.

Designing for missed time means choosing systems that can hold steady without constant correction. It means accepting that absence will happen and preparing for it rather than resisting it.

A garden designed for forgiveness does not panic when attention shifts. It waits.

The Grateful Hearts Solution

The Grateful Hearts Givings Garden is built to endure absence.

Self-watering systems sustain plants through dry days. Healthy soil retains moisture and nutrients. Contained beds slow the spread of weeds. Thoughtful plant choices recover after neglect.

These elements work together to create stability. The garden remains intact even when care is interrupted.

This design removes fear. It allows the gardener to step away without guilt.

Design Truth

A garden that collapses when unattended is not resilient.

Design truth reminds us that continuity depends on preparation, not presence. Systems that forgive absence protect both the harvest and the gardener's peace.

A garden should support life, not compete with it.

Practical Pause

Think about the last time you missed time in the garden.

What suffered first?
What held steady?
What recovered on its own?

Those answers reveal where forgiveness is present—and where it is missing.

Bringing It Together

Gardens designed to endure absence remain welcoming.

They do not punish missed days or shame missed seasons. They resume when the gardener returns, ready to continue without resentment.

A garden that forgives time is a garden that understands life—and serves it faithfully.

Chapter Fourteen

Passing the Garden Forward

Every garden eventually reaches a moment when someone else must step in.

It may happen gradually or all at once. A helping hand becomes necessary. A responsibility is shared. Care shifts from one person to another. This transition is not failure. It is part of continuity.

A garden designed to be passed forward carries its purpose beyond one pair of hands.

The Hidden Problem

The hidden problem is designing gardens that only one person understands.

When systems rely on memory, habit, or personal routine, they become fragile. Even well-meaning helpers hesitate when they cannot tell what belongs where or how care is meant to continue.

This turns transition into disruption. Instead of being carried forward, the garden stalls.

The Design Shift

The design shift begins when clarity replaces control.

Designing for succession means creating systems that speak for themselves. Clear layouts, visible functions, and repeatable processes allow others to step in without instruction.

The garden no longer belongs to one person's knowledge. It becomes understandable, transferable, and stable.

The Grateful Hearts Solution

The Grateful Hearts Givings Garden is designed with continuity in mind.

Modular beds define responsibility. Self-watering systems reduce decision-making. Consistent layouts remove confusion. Anyone can learn the rhythm quickly and continue the work without fear of undoing what came before.

This design allows care to move from person to person without interruption.

Design Truth

A garden that cannot be passed forward is temporary by design.

Longevity depends on accessibility—not just physical, but practical. When systems are simple and visible, care becomes shareable.

Design truth reminds us that stewardship includes preparing for succession.

Practical Pause

Imagine someone else tending your garden tomorrow.

Would they know what to water?
Would they understand what to harvest?
Would they feel confident continuing the work?

If the answer is unclear, the design may need refinement.

Bringing It Together

Passing the garden forward is an act of trust.

When design allows others to step in seamlessly, the garden outlives individual capacity. It continues to serve, provide, and grow without disruption.

A garden designed for succession becomes a gift—one that carries purpose forward with grace.

Chapter Fifteen

The Garden That Outlives the Gardener

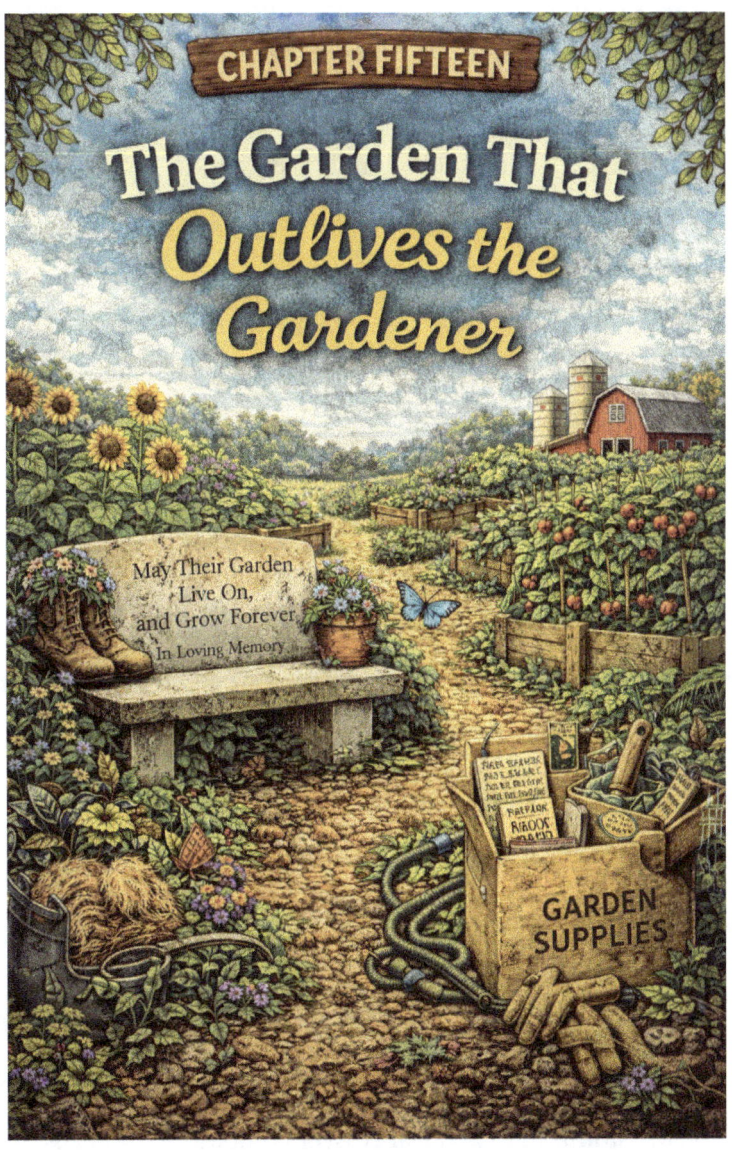

Some gardens are tied tightly to the people who built them.

When the gardener steps away, the garden fades with them.

Others continue quietly. They grow, produce, and serve without needing explanation. Their presence remains steady, even when the original hands are no longer there to tend them.

The difference is not devotion. It is design.

The Hidden Problem

The hidden problem is believing that longevity comes from commitment alone.

Gardens that depend on constant personal oversight rarely survive transition. When care becomes too specific, too complex, or too dependent on one person's strength and memory, continuity becomes fragile.

Eventually, the garden ends—not because it was unloved, but because it was impossible to sustain without its creator.

The Design Shift

The design shift happens when the goal moves beyond personal use.

Designing a garden to outlive the gardener means choosing systems that function independently. It means valuing simplicity over customization and clarity over complexity. It means planning for care by others without requiring interpretation or translation.

This shift allows the garden's purpose to extend beyond one season or one lifetime.

The Grateful Hearts Solution

The Grateful Hearts Givings Garden is built for endurance.

Its systems are visible. Its care is intuitive. Its layout invites continuity rather than confusion. Watering, harvesting, and maintenance are clear enough for anyone willing to help.

This design does not erase the gardener's presence. It honors it by ensuring the work continues.

Design Truth

A garden that lasts beyond the gardener is not accidental.

Longevity is the result of thoughtful choices made early. When design supports clarity, access, and shared responsibility, the garden becomes resilient to change.

Design truth reminds us that legacy is built through structure, not control.

Practical Pause

Consider what would remain if you were no longer present.

Would the garden still function?
Would its purpose still be clear?
Would its care still be possible?

These questions are not about absence. They are about preparation.

Bringing It Together

A garden that outlives the gardener carries forward intention.

It continues to feed, to teach, and to serve without needing to be explained. It stands as evidence that thoughtful design can extend care beyond personal capacity.

This is not about leaving something behind.
It is about building something that remains.

Chapter Sixteen
A Garden That Serves, Not Demands

Some gardens ask constantly.

They ask for time that is not always available, energy that is not always present, and attention that cannot always be given. Over time, those requests become expectations. And expectations quietly become burdens.

A garden that serves does not ask to be carried. It offers support instead.

The Hidden Problem

The hidden problem is the belief that commitment must feel heavy to be faithful.

Gardeners often accept exhaustion as proof of dedication. They assume that struggle means the work matters. When the garden becomes overwhelming, they push harder instead of questioning the design.

But a system that demands constant sacrifice is not sustainable. It eventually takes more than it gives.

The Design Shift

The design shift happens when service becomes the measure of success.

A garden designed to serve considers how it gives back—to the gardener's body, to their time, and to their peace. It asks whether the work feels restorative or depleting, supportive or demanding.

This shift allows the gardener to release guilt and embrace wisdom. The goal is no longer to keep up, but to remain in relationship.

The Grateful Hearts Solution

The Grateful Hearts Givings Garden is built on service.

Its systems reduce strain. Its layout invites help. Its care routines fit into real life. The garden offers food, beauty, and purpose without requiring constant negotiation.

This design allows the gardener to show up fully without being consumed by the work. The garden becomes a partner rather than a task.

Design Truth

A garden that serves does not require proving worth through effort.

When design supports ease, continuity follows. When systems function quietly in the background, attention can be given where it matters most.

Design truth reminds us that sustainability is felt, not measured.

Practical Pause

Take a moment to reflect on how your garden makes you feel.

Do you approach it with anticipation or obligation?
Does it restore you or drain you?
Does it fit into your life, or does your life bend around it?

These questions reveal whether service is flowing in the right direction.

Bringing It Together

A garden that serves does more than grow food.

It supports the person who tends it. It invites others to share in the work. It continues through change without demanding explanation or endurance.

What once sounded like an age-related idea revealed itself as something deeper—a reminder that good design is simply kindness extended into the future.

When a garden is designed with care for both land and life, it becomes what it was always meant to be—a steady presence, a quiet helper, and a lasting gift.

And that is the heart of the Grateful Hearts Givings Garden.

A Word About What Comes Next

This book was written to stand on its own.

If you never build another bed, adjust another container, or change another system, the ideas here have already done their work. They have asked you to think differently about how gardens fit into real lives.

But this garden does not exist in isolation.

Designing a garden that serves you creates space for something larger to emerge—sharing, giving, and continuity beyond the garden fence. When a garden becomes sustainable for the gardener, it becomes possible to extend that sustainability outward.

What comes next is not more work. It is a widening of purpose.

The principles in this book naturally lead toward questions of fairness, responsibility, and ethical sharing. Those questions are explored more fully in the next volume of this series, where the focus shifts from the garden itself to the harvest it produces and how that harvest is shared with dignity.

For now, it is enough to let this garden stand as it is—steady, thoughtful, and prepared.

Garden Wisdom

Gardens teach quietly.

They reveal what lasts and what does not. They respond honestly to design, care, and neglect. They do not hurry to impress, and they do not demand explanations.

A well-designed garden does not need to be defended. It proves itself over time.

The wisdom of a garden is found not in how much it produces, but in how consistently it serves. When the systems are sound, the work becomes lighter. When the design is thoughtful, the garden becomes forgiving.

Gardens remind us that sustainability is not about control. It is about relationship.

What you have learned here is not limited to soil, containers, or water. It applies wherever care, effort, and responsibility must be sustained over time.

Final Reflection

This book began with a simple idea: that a garden should serve the person tending it.

That idea has guided every chapter, every principle, and every design choice explored here. It is an idea rooted in dignity—dignity for the body, for time, and for the seasons of life that arrive without warning.

A garden designed with foresight becomes a place of peace instead of pressure. It adapts instead of resists. It continues instead of collapses.

As you close this book, remember that good design is an act of kindness extended into the future. It is a way of caring not just for plants, but for yourself and for those who may one day step in beside you.

May the garden you build serve you well.
May it remain gentle, steady, and generous.
And may it continue long after the work of building is done.

A Transition Into What We Owe the Harvest

This book focused on the garden itself—how it is designed, how it serves the person tending it, and how it remains steady through change.

But a well-designed garden does not stop at sustainability.

When a garden begins to produce consistently, new questions emerge. Not questions of technique, but of responsibility. What is grown matters less than how it is handled, shared, and given. Harvest introduces moral weight. It brings choice, intention, and consequence into view.

A garden that serves the gardener prepares the ground for something larger. It creates the conditions for fairness. It makes it possible to give without strain, to share without waste, and to distribute without harm.

The next book turns toward those questions.

It explores what happens after the garden works—after food is harvested, after abundance appears, and after giving becomes possible. It asks how faith, dignity, and ethics guide the sharing of what the land provides.

Design made sustainability possible.
Harvest now asks for wisdom.

That is where the work continues.

The principles explored in this book are rooted in design that lasts—gardens that remain usable as seasons change, strength shifts, and needs evolve. While philosophy provides the foundation, systems give it form. What follows is not a separate idea, but a practical companion to the approach you have just read. The pages ahead document a mobile, self-watering garden system developed to reflect the same values of accessibility, longevity, and thoughtful care. It exists to show how these principles can be carried forward, one contained space at a time.

Companion Section

Mobile Milk Crate Gardening

*A Practical Companion to
The Grateful Hearts Givings Garden*

Invented and written by **JoAnn Comer-Conwell**

Mobile Milk Crate Gardening

This booklet documents a simple, mobile, self-watering garden system developed through lived experience, necessity, and long-term use. It exists to support gardeners who need systems that adapt to real life—changing strength, changing seasons, limited space, and the responsibility of caring for both plants and people. This is not a trend method.

It is a working system.

This booklet explains Mobile Milk Crate Gardening,

a self-watering, mobile container gardening system invented by JoAnn Comer-Conwell.

The system uses stacked milk crates, a water reservoir, and air-pruning principles to grow vegetables, herbs, and even trees in a way that is affordable, accessible, and scalable. It was designed to support gardeners of all ages, including seniors, volunteers, and those with limited space or strength, while producing healthy plants and reliable harvests indoors or outdoors.

Clarifying the Design

Gardening in milk crates has existed in many forms, and the basic principle of wicking water is not new. I do not claim to have invented milk crate gardening or wicking itself.

What I did develop—and have not seen documented elsewhere—is a two-crate, mobile, self-watering system where water is stored in a lower milk crate and intentionally wicked upward into a separate growing crate above. This double-crate design makes the system easier to move in parts, supports consistent moisture, and allows plants to benefit from airflow and healthier root development.

Single milk crate planters are common. This booklet documents a different solution: a repeatable structure that combines mobility, self-watering from crate to crate, and long-term usability in one simple build.

Why This System Exists

Many gardens fail not because people stop caring, but because the garden requires more effort each year to maintain. Heavy watering, constant bending, inconsistent moisture, and rigid placement quietly drain both energy and joy.

Mobile Milk Crate Gardening was created to remove those barriers while preserving plant health, dignity, and continuity.

The two milk crates were free from a store that was throwing them away.

The blue bucket came from the Dollar Tree store.

The two stripes of wicking material is 1-inch wide, white nylon

Each milk crate is lined with breathable weed block

A Garden That Moves With You

Gardens are often built as permanent fixtures. Life, however, is not permanent in the same way. Strength fluctuates. Light shifts. Needs change.

This system allows the garden to move-into the sun, out of the heat, closer to a door, under a light, or away from strain - without dismantling the plant itself.

Designed for Every Stage of Life

This system supports gardeners of all ages. Children can observe and learn. Adults can scale and expand. Seniors can tend without excessive bending or lifting.

It is not age-specific.
It is life-aware.

Milk crate gardening naturally breaks growing food down into manageable pieces. Each milk crate measures approximately eleven inches by eleven inches—close enough to a single square foot to be treated as one. That detail matters more than it may seem.

When gardening is approached one square foot at a time, the mind responds differently. Instead of seeing rows, beds, or an overwhelming workload, the focus narrows to a single, contained space. One crate. One plant. One small area that can be observed, tended, and completed without strain.

This changes how gardening feels.

Rather than thinking, *I have an entire garden to manage*, the work becomes, *I only need to take care of this one crate right now*. That shift reduces mental fatigue and physical pressure. Even when a garden contains dozens—or even hundreds—of milk crates, the task remains the same. One square foot at a time.

This approach makes large gardens possible without making them overwhelming. Whether someone is caring for three crates or three hundred, the method does not change. Attention moves from crate to crate, slowly and intentionally. Before long, the entire garden has been tended—often more easily than expected.

Because the crates are raised and mobile, much of this care can be done while seated. A bench placed along the path allows the gardener to work at eye level, reducing strain and encouraging observation rather than haste. Leaves are noticed. Soil moisture is checked. Small changes are addressed early.

This is what I refer to as **"Gardening Therapy"**.

Not therapy in a clinical sense, but in the way steady, purposeful care restores calm. The repetition is gentle. The scale is manageable. The results are visible. Gardening becomes relaxing rather than demanding, healthy rather than exhausting, and life-giving rather than draining.

When gardening is designed this way, it supports both the plants and the person tending them.

Cost Should Not Be a Barrier

Mobile Milk Crate Gardening was intentionally designed using materials that are accessible, inexpensive, and familiar. This system does not rely on specialty containers, proprietary parts, or replacement components that must be purchased repeatedly over time. It was built to work with what people can reasonably obtain, not what they are pressured to buy.

Many traditional gardening systems quietly assume disposable income. Raised beds, custom planters, branded self-watering containers, and replacement inserts often carry ongoing costs that make long-term growing unrealistic for people on fixed incomes, tight budgets, or limited resources. Over time, these costs discourage consistency and lead many gardeners to abandon growing food altogether.

This system was designed to avoid that outcome.

Milk crates themselves are widely available. In many communities, they can be obtained at little or no cost through local grocery stores, bakeries, or distributors that discard damaged or excess crates. While not every location allows reuse, many crates are removed from circulation and would otherwise be thrown away. When available through legitimate means, these crates become a practical foundation for growing food rather than waste.

Even when free crates are not available, the cost remains intentionally low. In most areas, a milk crate can be purchased for under six dollars at a local big-box or hardware store. Because the system uses only two crates per growing unit, the total structural cost remains modest and predictable. There are no proprietary pieces that require replacement, and no specialty containers that must be upgraded or reordered.

The design also allows gardeners to build slowly. One crate can be added at a time. Systems can be expanded as resources allow, rather than requiring a large upfront investment. This makes the system accessible to individuals, families, churches, and community groups alike.

Gardening should not depend on disposable income.
Food access should not depend on strength, speed, or constant spending.

This system respects those realities. It was created so that the ability to grow food is determined by intention and care—not by how much money someone can afford to put into a container.

Indoor and Outdoor Use

This system functions indoors or outdoors. It adapts to windows, porches, patios, yards, grow lights, and community spaces.

One design.
Multiple environments.

What Is Mobile Milk Crate Gardening?

It is a self-watering container garden built using stacked milk crates. A water reservoir sits below the soil chamber, allowing moisture to wick upward as needed.

The plant controls the water intake.
The gardener controls placement.

How Self-Watering Works

Water is stored separately from the soil. A wicking material draws moisture upward gradually, maintaining consistent hydration without oversaturation.

This reduces stress on the plant and eliminates daily watering labor.

Why Self-Watering Matters

Plants thrive when moisture is consistent. Dry-wet cycles weaken roots and reduce nutrient uptake.

Self-watering supports steady growth, stronger roots, and healthier yields.

Materials Required

Two milk crates
One small bucket
One nylon stocking or other (wicking material)
Two yards of weed block fabric
One 13-gallon kitchen trash bag
Approximately six gallons of nutrient-dense wicking soil

Optional Adaptations

Garden stakes for support
Water-resistant outer fabric
Additional bracing for wind exposure

These adaptations expand the system without altering its core design.

Why These Materials Matter

Every material used in the Mobile Milk Crate Gardening system was chosen intentionally. The design is practical, but it is not short-term, improvised, or disposable. Each component supports plant health, gardener comfort, and long-term use under real-life conditions.

Milk crates are often misunderstood as temporary or utilitarian objects, but in reality, they are built for durability. The hard plastic used to manufacture milk crates was engineered to withstand extreme abuse. These crates were originally designed to carry heavy glass milk bottles—items that were stacked, transported, dropped, and handled roughly day after day. The material had to endure weight, impact, moisture, and constant movement without cracking or deforming.

As a result, milk crates are exceptionally long-lasting. When used in a garden setting, they do not break down, rot, or require replacement. A properly sourced milk crate can last a lifetime. This durability makes them ideal for systems intended to remain functional across many seasons and changing physical abilities.

While milk crates may not appear decorative at first glance, appearance was never the driving purpose behind their use. That said, they can be adapted aesthetically if desired lined, skirted, grouped intentionally, or incorporated into an organized garden layout. Visual refinement is optional. The system does not rely on appearance to perform well.

Milk crates are used in this system because they are convenient in a meaningful way. Their uniform size makes them easy to handle one at a time. A single crate can be set up, planted, or adjusted without lifting excessive weight or committing to a large, permanent structure. This allows gardeners to build gradually, expand at their own pace, and respond to changing needs without strain.

Their open-sided structure allows air to circulate around the soil chamber, supporting healthier root systems and preventing moisture from becoming trapped. Their strength allows them to be stacked securely, creating elevation without instability. Their consistency allows gardeners to observe and maintain each growing space with clarity.

Today, milk crates are used far beyond their original purpose. Businesses often use them to transport food and supplies before removing them from circulation. When obtained responsibly, these crates can be redirected from waste into long-term food production.

The materials in this system were chosen to endure—not to impress, not to be replaced, and not to wear out. They exist to support a garden that remains usable, reliable, and steady over time.

Air Root Pruning & Root Health by Design

Plant health begins below the surface. While leaves and stems show visible signs of growth, it is the root system that determines how well a plant absorbs nutrients, manages water, and withstands stress over time. A strong root system supports everything above it.

Air root pruning is a natural process that occurs when a growing root reaches air exposure. When the root tip encounters air, it dries and stops extending outward. This does not harm the plant. Instead, the plant responds by producing additional lateral roots behind the stopped tip. Over time, this creates a dense, fibrous root system rather than a few long, wandering roots.

This distinction matters.

In many traditional containers, roots grow until they hit a solid wall, then turn and continue circling the container. These circling roots compete with one another, restrict nutrient uptake, and interfere with water movement. As the plant matures, this can lead to uneven moisture, increased susceptibility to rot and disease, and reduced productivity. Root-bound stress often goes unnoticed until the plant begins to decline.

Air root pruning interrupts that cycle.

When roots are encouraged to branch instead of circle, they distribute themselves more evenly throughout the soil. This improves nutrient absorption, stabilizes moisture levels, and strengthens the plant's overall structure. Healthy roots support healthy growth above the soil line. Root health determines plant health.

The Mobile Milk Crate Gardening system supports air root pruning through structure rather than intervention. Milk crates naturally allow airflow around the soil chamber when lined correctly. As roots grow outward, they encounter air at the crate's edges and respond by branching inward. No mechanical pruning, chemicals, or specialized containers are required.

In this way, the crate itself becomes part of the plant's health system.

This design produces several long-term benefits. Plants experience reduced transplant shock because roots are already well-distributed. Fruiting plants often show increased yield due to improved nutrient uptake. Recovery after movement or environmental stress is faster because the root system remains balanced. Root disease and rot are less likely to develop because excess moisture does not become trapped. Soil moisture remains more even throughout the container rather than pooling in one area.

Most importantly, this process happens quietly. Once the system is built, air root pruning continues on its own. The gardener does not need to intervene. The plant responds naturally to the environment created by thoughtful design.

When roots are allowed to grow as they were designed to grow—branching, breathing, and balancing—the plant above reflects that strength. Growth becomes steadier. Maintenance becomes easier. The garden becomes more resilient.

Air root pruning in this system is not an added feature. It is the result of intentional structure.

Reduced Bending and Strain

Stacked crates raise the growing surface. This minimizes bending and allows seated or standing care.

Gardening should not injure the gardener.

Visibility and Awareness

Elevated containers make it easier to see leaves, stems, and soil conditions. Problems are noticed early, before damage spreads.

Observation replaces reaction.

Reduction by Elevation

Raising plants off the ground reduces access for crawling pests and soil-borne issues.

Design becomes protection.

Moving the System Safely

Mobility in this system is not about convenience. It is about protection—of both the plants and the person tending them.

Gardens are often designed as if nothing will ever need to change. Sun exposure is assumed to be permanent. Strength is assumed to be constant. Weather is treated as predictable. In reality, gardens must respond to shifting conditions, and gardeners must respond to changing bodies.

The Mobile Milk Crate Gardening system allows movement without disruption. Because the system is built in parts, no single lift carries unnecessary weight. Soil, water, and structure can be handled separately, reducing strain and minimizing risk.

If a crate needs to be moved into shade during extreme heat, it can be done without uprooting the plant. If weather requires temporary shelter, the system can be relocated gradually. Indoors or outdoors, the garden adapts rather than resists change.

This flexibility is especially important for older gardeners, caregivers, and volunteers. Mobility reduces injury, prevents burnout, and encourages continued engagement rather than abandonment. When movement is possible, gardeners remain willing to tend rather than feeling trapped by the garden itself.

A garden that cannot move eventually demands more than it gives.

A garden that can move continues to serve.

Mobility & Aging-in-Place

Gardens are often designed for the moment they are built, not for the years that follow. Beds are placed low, pathways are narrow, and access assumes consistent strength and flexibility. Over time, these assumptions quietly fail.

Aging-in-place gardening requires a different approach.

The Mobile Milk Crate Gardening system was designed to remain usable as bodies change. Mobility is not treated as an upgrade or convenience—it is built into the structure itself. Crates can be raised, lowered, spaced, and moved to meet the gardener where they are physically, rather than demanding the gardener adapt to the garden.

Because each unit is self-contained, adjustments can be made gradually. A crate can be moved closer to a door. Another can be raised higher. Work can be done seated rather than standing. None of these changes require rebuilding the garden or abandoning the plants.

This flexibility allows people to continue growing food even as strength, balance, or endurance shifts. It also allows caregivers and volunteers to assist without taking control away from the gardener. Independence is preserved alongside support.

A garden that supports aging-in-place does more than produce food.

It preserves dignity.

By designing for mobility from the beginning, the system removes the need for sudden transitions later. Gardening does not end when conditions change. It simply adjusts.

This is how gardens remain part of daily life rather than something people must eventually give up.

Respecting the Weight of Water

Water is heavy. By isolating the reservoir, this system reduces strain and protects both plants and bodies.

This is intentional design.

What You Can Grow

Vegetables
Herbs
Leafy greens
Fruit-bearing plants

Most garden plants adapt well to this system.

Growing Trees in Milk Crates

Trees can be grown and maintained in this system with proper pruning and care. Growth is controlled, not forced.

Longevity matters more than size.

Bonsai as Possibility

This system allows trees to be intentionally shaped and maintained at manageable sizes, supporting patience and long-term observation.

Small does not mean limited.

Scaling the System

One crate can become many. Systems can be duplicated without changing methods.

Consistency allows expansion.

Donation Gardens & Redirection from Waste

Donation gardens succeed or fail based on one simple factor: sustainability. Not whether people care, not whether the need exists, but whether the system can continue when enthusiasm fades, volunteers change, or resources become limited.

The Mobile Milk Crate Gardening system was developed with these realities in mind.

Traditional donation gardens often depend on permanent land, heavy infrastructure, and consistent physical labor. When access to land changes, when a key volunteer steps away, or when maintenance becomes too demanding, the garden quietly disappears. Food production stops not because the mission failed, but because the system could not adapt.

This system was designed to adapt.

Because milk crate gardens are mobile, food can be grown where people already live—near senior housing, community centers, churches, schools, and shared spaces. The garden does not need to be built once and left behind. It can be relocated, reconfigured, or temporarily paused without destroying the plants or abandoning the effort.

Mobility also protects volunteers. Tasks can be divided. Crates can be tended one at a time. Work can be shared among people of different abilities without placing the burden on a few strong individuals. This allows donation gardens to remain active even as volunteer availability changes.

Just as important is the system's relationship to waste.

Milk crates are built to last, yet many are removed from circulation once they are no longer needed for commercial transport. Businesses use them to move food and supplies, then discard or replace them. When responsibly sourced, these crates represent durable material already in existence—material that does not need to be newly manufactured in order to grow food.

Redirecting these crates into food production gives them a second purpose that is both practical and meaningful. Instead of becoming waste, they become containers for nourishment. Instead of occupying storage or landfills, they support growing, sharing, and feeding.

This redirection matters.

Donation gardens often operate with limited budgets. By using materials that already exist, the system reduces startup costs while increasing durability. Resources can be directed toward seeds, soil, and distribution rather than infrastructure that must be rebuilt every season.

The system also supports continuity. Crates can be labeled, tracked, and reassigned. When one location can no longer host a garden, the system moves with the mission. Food production does not depend on a single site or a single season.

In this way, Mobile Milk Crate Gardening aligns with a broader ethic of stewardship—of resources, of people, and of effort. Nothing is wasted unnecessarily. Nothing is built to be abandoned. The system exists to support long-term giving, not short-term projects.

A donation garden should not disappear when conditions change. It should remain—adaptable, movable, and ready to serve wherever it is needed next.

Seed Access and Community Support

A garden system is only as sustainable as the resources that support it. While soil, containers, and structure form the foundation, seeds determine whether a garden can begin again—season after season.

Many donation gardens struggle because seed access is inconsistent. When seeds must be purchased repeatedly, limited budgets are quickly exhausted. When varieties change unpredictably, planning becomes difficult. Over time, this instability weakens even the most well-intentioned efforts.

The Mobile Milk Crate Gardening system was designed to work well within partnerships that already exist.

Some seed companies, local garden centers, agricultural programs, and community organizations offer free or discounted seeds to support donation gardens and food-growing initiatives. When gardens are built on simple, repeatable systems, these partnerships become immediately usable rather than aspirational. Seeds can be planted the same day they are received. No specialized infrastructure is required.

This system also supports seed stewardship. Because crates are uniform and portable, they can be labeled, tracked, and rotated with ease. Gardeners can observe which varieties perform well, save seeds when appropriate, and gradually build resilience into the garden itself. Knowledge accumulates alongside harvests.

Partnerships are strengthened when systems are reliable. When donors, volunteers, or organizations see food consistently produced and shared, trust grows. The garden becomes something others are willing to support because it demonstrates responsibility rather than dependency.

Seed access is not only about planting.
It is about continuity.

When seeds, systems, and partnerships work together, food production becomes steady rather than seasonal. The garden does not restart from scratch each year—it continues.

Placement and Light Awareness

Plants communicate through growth. This system allows gardeners to respond by adjusting placement rather than forcing conditions. Movement replaces struggle.

Learning to Listen

Healthy gardening begins with observation. This system creates space to notice patterns instead of reacting to failure.

Attention becomes care.

Consistency Over Perfection

Gardens do not fail because people lack knowledge. They fail because systems require more effort than can be sustained over time.

Perfection-driven gardening demands constant correction—exact watering schedules, precise feeding routines, rigid layouts, and continual upgrades. While these methods may appear efficient on paper, they rarely survive real life.

The Mobile Milk Crate Gardening system was designed with consistency in mind, not perfection. It allows small, repeated actions to accumulate into lasting results. Watering becomes predictable. Observation replaces urgency. Problems are addressed early rather than after damage occurs.

Because the system supports steady habits, it encourages gardeners to return. A garden that feels manageable is more likely to be tended regularly. A garden that demands precision often becomes neglected.

Consistency builds trust—between the gardener and the system, and between the system and the plants. Over time, this trust produces healthier growth, stronger yields, and a calmer relationship with the work itself.

Gardening is not meant to be mastered.
It is meant to be maintained.

Not a Shortcut Garden

This is not about speed or convenience. It is about sustainability, protection, and respect for effort.

Thoughtful gardens endure.

Gardening That Honors Limits

This system aligns with the principle of designing gardens that remain functional even when strength changes.

Design carries the work forward.

Quiet Stewardship

Not all work needs to be visible to be valuable.

Much of gardening happens without witnesses—watering quietly, checking leaves, noticing small changes that never become problems because they were seen early. This kind of stewardship does not draw attention, but it sustains life.

The Mobile Milk Crate Gardening system supports this quiet work. It does not demand constant adjustment or correction. Instead, it creates space for observation, patience, and care practiced at a human pace.

Stewardship in this context is not about control.
It is about responsibility.

It is choosing systems that do not exhaust people.
It is designing gardens that remain when effort pauses.
It is valuing consistency over display.

When gardens are built this way, they become places of calm rather than pressure. The work becomes grounding. The harvest becomes shared. The effort becomes part of daily rhythm rather than an added burden.

Quiet stewardship does not rush.
It does not compete.
It does not demand recognition.

It simply continues.

What This Garden Asks of You

This garden does not ask for speed.

It does not ask for strength beyond what you have, or energy you must borrow from tomorrow. It does not demand constant attention, perfect timing, or uninterrupted effort. It does not require you to prove anything.

What it asks for is presence.

A moment to notice soil moisture.
A pause to observe leaves.
A willingness to return, even briefly, when you can.

This kind of garden does not reward urgency. It responds instead to consistency—small acts repeated gently over time. One crate checked. One plant watered. One decision made without pressure.

You do not have to finish everything at once.
You do not have to keep up with anyone else's pace.

The design carries part of the work for you. It holds water when you cannot. It supports roots without constant correction. It remains steady when your attention must move elsewhere.

In doing so, the garden gives something back.

It offers rhythm instead of demand.
Care instead of strain.
A place where effort is never wasted, even when it is small.

This garden asks only what is reasonable.
And it gives more than it takes.

When the Garden Is Quiet

There are times when the garden is active, and times when it is quiet.

Quiet does not mean neglected.
Quiet does not mean abandoned.
Quiet does not mean failed.

Quiet is simply a pause.

In many systems, a pause causes collapse. Water runs out. Roots suffer. Progress is lost. The garden becomes something that must be rescued or rebuilt.

This system was created to allow quiet without consequence.

When the garden is still, water remains available. Roots continue to hold. The structure stays intact. The work you have already done is preserved rather than undone.

This matters more than it seems.

Life does not move in straight lines. Strength fluctuates. Responsibilities interrupt. Seasons change. A garden that can withstand quiet moments becomes a companion rather than an obligation.

It waits without reproach.
It remains without complaint.

And when you return—whether after a day, a week, or longer—the garden is still there. Ready. Steady. Continuing the work it was designed to do.

A garden that honors quiet honors the gardener as well.

A Garden That Remains

A garden should not disappear when effort pauses.

Many gardens depend on constant motion. When energy slows, when hands are absent, or when life interrupts routine, those gardens decline quickly. Beds dry out. Plants struggle. The work becomes something that must be restarted rather than continued.

This system was designed for a different outcome.

A garden that remains is one that does not demand urgency. It continues quietly, supported by structure rather than force. Water remains available. Roots remain healthy. The garden holds itself steady until care resumes.

This kind of garden respects real life. It allows for rest, recovery, and interruption without loss. It does not punish absence. It does not require perfection. It simply continues.

Faithful systems are not loud. They do not rely on constant correction or attention. They are built with foresight, allowing small efforts to carry forward even when hands are temporarily still.

In this way, the garden becomes a companion rather than a burden.

The Mobile Milk Crate Gardening system exists to support this continuity. It was created so that food production does not collapse when strength changes or circumstances shift. It allows gardens to persist through seasons, transitions, and time itself.

A garden that remains does more than grow food.
It holds space for care, patience, and return.

That is the purpose of this system.

About the Author

JoAnn Comer-Conwell is a faith-rooted gardener, teacher, and nonprofit founder whose work focuses on ethical food growing, accessible garden design, and dignity-centered food sharing. She is the founder of Grateful Hearts Givings NJ Nonprofit (501)(c)(3), where she leads community-based efforts to grow and distribute real food in ways that honor God, respect people, and protect the labor behind every harvest.

Through hands-on gardening, education, and community partnerships, JoAnn helps individuals and organizations learn how to grow chemical-free food using sustainable, senior-friendly systems, even when starting with limited space, resources, or physical strength. Her work emphasizes long-term garden planning, accessible design, self-watering systems, and ethical stewardship as foundations for lasting abundance.

JoAnn's gardening philosophy is shaped by lived experience—working on borrowed land, organizing shared gardens, feeding those in need, and building systems that continue to function even when time, energy, or help is limited. She believes food should be grown the way God intended: thoughtfully, honestly, and with care for both the earth and the people it serves.

She lives and gardens in New Jersey, where her work through Grateful Hearts Givings NJ Nonprofit focuses especially on senior citizens and individuals facing food insecurity, offering practical pathways to healthier food and more sustainable living.

About Grateful Hearts Givings NJ Nonprofit

Grateful Hearts Givings NJ Nonprofit exists to restore trust in food, dignity in service, and integrity in stewardship.

Through community gardens, education, and outreach, the nonprofit works to ensure that food is grown and shared with care, clarity, and respect. Its mission centers on ethical growing practices, fair distribution, and systems that protect both people and land, with a special commitment to senior citizens and those experiencing food insecurity.

The organization's work is rooted in practical action—growing food, sharing harvests, teaching sustainable methods, and building partnerships that support long-term access to nourishing food. Every garden, lesson, and act of service is guided by faith, gratitude, and responsibility.

This book is one extension of that mission.

Grow slowly.
Grow wisely.
Grow with grateful hearts.

All titles can be found on
amazon.com

under author
JoAnn Comer-Conwell

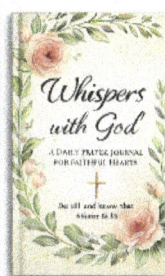

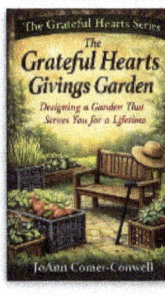
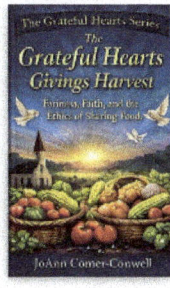

www.ingramcontent.com/pod-product-compliance
Lightning Source LLC
Chambersburg PA
CBHW050112170426
43198CB00014B/2550